Roseo

CW00517932

English Grammar

by CEFR Levels

For English Learners, Teachers, and Materials Developers

Z. Smith

English Grammar by CEFR Levels
for English Learners, Teachers, and Materials Developers
by Z. Smith

Copyright © 2023 Zoe Smith
The right of Zoe Smith to be identified as the author of this work has been asserted by her in accordance with the Copyright, Designs and Patents Act 1988. All rights reserved. This book is sold subject to the condition that it shall not, by way of trade or otherwise, be lent, re-sold, hired out or otherwise circulated in any form of binding or cover other than that in which it is published and without a similar condition including this condition being imposed on the subsequent purchaser.

Publisher: Z-proof Editorial Services
Cover design and editing: Z-proof Editorial Services
https://zproofeditorial.wordpress.com/

ISBN: 978-1-7393610-0-6 paperback

CONTENTS

vi

ABOUT THE CEFR AND THIS BOOK

This grammar book is uniquely organized by the positioning of grammar items according to difficulty, as identified by the Common European Framework of Reference for Languages (CEFR). The CEFR is a standardized system that is based on six levels of proficiency: A1 and A2 (beginner), B1 and B2 (intermediate), C1 and C2 (advanced). Each level is defined by a set of descriptors that describe what a learner can do in the four language skills of reading, writing, speaking, and listening. Areas such as grammar by CEFR level are listed in sources such as the *British Council/EAQUALS Core Inventory for General English* and https://www.englishprofile.org/english-grammar-profile/egp-online.

My book is intended as a concise grammar reference book, aimed at:

Learners of English: Learners can use the book to check that they have covered all of the grammar areas appropriate to their CEFR level. They can also use it to see which grammatical structures they still need to master to be able to score more highly in an English test.

Teachers of English: This book can be used as a handy refresher to help explain the most salient points of a grammar feature to learners. It could be especially useful for teachers on a CELTA/TESOL training course who need to get to grips with unfamiliar grammatical terms.

Materials developers: Want to have an overview of where grammatical items stand relative to the progression of learner abilities? Use this book to help sequence the grammar items in your materials.

Many of the grammar points in this book are accompanied by short exercises to help consolidate the main ideas of those grammar points. At the back of the book, there are also some ideas for classroom activities that teachers can give learners to help practice the different past tenses.

In the author's experience, the three grammar areas that nearly all learners struggle to demonstrate competency in and which need extra practice are:

- the present perfect
- the passive
- mixed conditionals

KEY GRAMMATICAL TERMS

Adjective: a word that modifies a noun or pronoun by describing or giving more information about it

Adverb: a word that modifies a verb, adjective, or another adverb by providing information on time, place, manner, degree, or frequency

Article: *a*, *an*, *the* – these are used to refer to nouns

Clause: a group of words that contains a subject and a predicate, and can stand alone as a sentence or be part of a larger sentence

Gerund: a verb form ending in *-ing* that functions as a noun

Infinitive: a verb form that usually begins with *to* and can function as a noun, adjective, or adverb

Noun: a word that refers to a person/animal, place, thing, or idea

Object: the noun or pronoun that receives the action of the verb

- **Direct object:** the noun or pronoun that receives the action of the verb directly
- **Indirect object:** the noun or pronoun that receives the direct object indirectly

Predicate: the part of the sentence that provides information about the subject and contains the verb

Preposition: a word that shows the relationship between a noun or pronoun and other words in the sentence by indicating position, direction, or time

Pronoun: a word used to replace a noun, often to avoid repetition

Subject: the noun or pronoun that performs the action or is the focus of the sentence

Tense: a form of the verb that indicates the time at which the action took place or will take place

Verb: a word that expresses an action or a state of being; verbs can be *regular* or *irregular*, and can take different forms depending on the subject and the tense

A1: Adjectives: common

Adjectives describe a characteristic or quality of a noun. For example, "the red apple" and "the red car" both use the adjective "red" to describe the color of the nouns *apple* and *car*.

More than one adjective can describe a noun. For example, "a big old brown wooden box" uses five adjectives. Adjectives should be in the order of[1]:

Quantity: one, two, three, half, a dozen, few

Opinion: beautiful, brave, bright, clean, heroic, valuable, strong, stubborn, delicious, tasty, popular

Size: big, small, tiny, large, miniature, massive, microscopic

Physical quality: dirty, rough, smooth, thin, untidy

Age: young, old, new, antique, ancient, modern, middle-aged

Color: red, blue, green, yellow, purple, pink, black, white, brown

Shape: round, square, rectangular, circular, triangular, oval, oblong, cylindrical, spherical, hexagonal, long, short

Origin: American, British, Chinese, French, Italian, Spanish

Material: wooden, plastic, metallic, glass, ceramic, cotton, silk, leather, woolen, synthetic

Qualifier/Purpose: collapsible, cooking, hunting, vampire, zip-up

If two adjectives from the same category are used, then you might see a comma between those adjectives.

Example:

- The brave, happy British knight wears a purple woolen elegant T-shirt.

---

[1] The author has seen some sources giving a different order.

Read the passage and answer the questions.

My sister has a beautiful house. It's a large, white house with a red roof. She keeps it very clean and tidy. In the living room, there are two comfortable sofas and a big TV. The kitchen is spacious with a long, wooden table and six chairs. In the bedrooms, there are soft, cozy beds with fluffy pillows and warm blankets. I love spending time in her house.

1. What kind of house does the sister have?

     a) A small brown house with a gray roof.

     b) A large white house with a red roof.

2. How does the sister keep her house?

     a) She keeps it very clean and tidy.

     b) She doesn't keep it clean and tidy.

3. What is in the living room?

     a) Two uncomfortable sofas and a small TV.

     b) Two comfortable sofas and a big TV.

4. What is in the kitchen?

     a) A small plastic table and four chairs.

     b) A spacious wooden table and six chairs.

5. What are the beds like in the bedrooms?

     a) Soft and cozy with fluffy pillows and warm blankets.

     b) Uncomfortable and hard.

Answers: 1. b); 2. a); 3. b); 4. b); 5. a)

A1: Adjectives: demonstratives

Demonstrative adjectives specify which <u>noun</u> they are describing. The demonstrative adjectives are *this, that, these,* and *those*:

- **This** <u>apple</u> is delicious. (singular noun, near)
- **That** <u>car</u> is fast. (singular noun, farther away)
- **These** <u>flowers</u> are beautiful. (plural noun, near)
- **Those** <u>small birds</u> are singing. (plural noun, farther away)

EXERCISE

Complete the sentences with a suitable demonstrative adjective.

1. _____ child is noisy.

2. _____ books are too long!

3. _____ car is very fast.

Answers: 1. This/That; 2. These/Those; 3. This/That

Demonstrative adjectives must modify a noun. **Demonstrative pronouns**[2], on the other hand, can stand alone. They might need more context for us to understand what they refer to.

Examples:

- **That** <u>box</u> is blue. (*That* is a demonstrative adjective because it goes before a <u>noun</u>)
- **This** might be painful. (demonstrative pronoun – the situation here *might* be a doctor talking to a patient)
- I like **those**. (demonstrative pronoun – the situation here *might* be someone looking at some shoes in a store)

---

[2] See also the A1 entry for Pronouns

A1: Adverbs of frequency

Adverbs of frequency indicate how often an action or event occurs. Some common adverbs of frequency in English include *always*, *usually*, *often*, *sometimes*, *rarely*, and *never*.

They are usually placed in front of the main verb, but when the main verb is *to be*, they can be placed <u>after</u> the verb.

Examples:

- I **always** wake up early.
- He is **usually** late for work.
- Are you **usually** late for work?
- I'm not **usually** late for work.
- They **often** go to the movies on Friday nights.
- I **sometimes** play soccer on the weekends.
- She **rarely** drinks coffee.
- I **never** eat meat.

Some adverbs of frequency like *daily*, *weekly*, *monthly*, and *yearly* are also time adverbials; they indicate the time frame of an action.

Examples:

- I exercise **daily**.
- We meet **weekly**.
- He gets a salary **monthly**.
- They go on vacation **yearly**.

1. Answer the questions.

1. How often do you go to the gym?

2. Do you usually eat breakfast in the morning?

3. Do you always remember your friends' birthdays?

4. Do you sometimes read books in your free time?

5. Do you rarely clean your home?

2. Underline the adverbs of frequency in the passage.

I usually wake up at 6:30 in the morning. I always brush my teeth and wash my face before eating breakfast. Sometimes I have toast and coffee, but other times I have cereal and milk. I never skip breakfast, because it's the most important meal of the day. After breakfast, I usually go to work. I work from 9:00 to 5:00, Monday through Friday. On weekends, I often go for a run in the park or meet friends for brunch. Occasionally, I go to the cinema or a concert in the evening. I rarely stay up late, because I need at least eight hours of sleep.

Answers: usually, always, sometimes, never, usually, often, occasionally, rarely

A1: Comparatives and superlatives

Comparatives and superlatives are forms of adjectives and adverbs used to compare and contrast the degree of an adjective or adverb.

Comparatives compare two things. They are formed by adding *er* (or *ier* after adjectives ending in *y*) to an adjective, or by using *more* before an adjective or adverb.

Examples:

- He is **taller** <u>than</u> his brother. (comparative of *tall*)
- She runs **faster** <u>than</u> her friend. (comparative of *fast*)
- My sister is **more intelligent** <u>than</u> me. (comparative of *intelligent*)
- He speaks **more fluently** <u>than</u> me. (comparative of *fluently*)

If two things have the same value, use the structure *as ... as ...*

Examples:

- You are **as** <u>tall</u> **as** the horse.
- That coat is **not as** <u>pretty</u> **as** this one.

Superlatives indicate the highest or lowest degree of an adjective or adverb. They are formed by adding *(i)est* to an adjective or by using *most* or *least* before an adjective or adverb. *The* is also used before the superlative.

Examples:

- He is <u>the</u> **tallest** person in the class. (superlative of *tall*)
- She is <u>the</u> **fastest** runner in the team. (superlative of *fast*)
- The movie was <u>the</u> **least interesting** I have ever seen. (superlative of *interesting*)

For some irregular comparatives and superlatives, you have to memorize them.

Examples:

- good, better, the best
- bad, worse, the worst
- far, farther/further, the farthest/the furthest
- old, older/elder, the oldest/the eldest

EXERCISE

Read the sentences and choose the correct answer.

1. Which is _____, a cat or a lion?

     a) big   b) bigger   c) biggest

2. Tom is _____ than his brother.

     a) tall   b) taller   c) tallest

3. I think English is _____ than French.

     a) easy   b) easier   c) easiest

4. This is the _____ book I've ever read.

     a) interesting   b) more interesting   c) most interesting

5. Which is _____, coffee or tea?

     a) popular   b) more popular   c) most popular

Answers: 1. b); 2. b); 3. b); 4. c); 5. b)

A1: *Going to*

(See also the A2 entry for Future time [will and going to]*)*

Going to is used to talk about future plans or intentions. It is formed by using the base form of the verb *to go* + the infinitive form of the main verb.

Examples:

- I am **going to** visit my grandparents next week.
- They are **going to** have a party next Saturday.
- He is **going to** study computer science next semester.

The structure *going to* can also be used to talk about predictions based on present evidence.

Examples:

- Look at the dark clouds. It's **going to** rain.
- She's got all her clothes packed. She's **going to** leave.

Going to can be replaced by the present continuous to indicate a near future plan or arrangement.

Examples:

- I'**m visiting** my grandparents next week.
- They'**re having** a party next Saturday.

Also, *going to* is sometimes replaced by *will* to indicate a future action that is less planned or less certain.

Examples:

- I **will** see you tomorrow.
- He **will** call you back later.

The structure *going to* is also used to show the continuity of an action that has been happening and will happen in the future.

Examples:

- I am going to be a doctor after I graduate. (the speaker is already on a medical degree course)
- They are going to be married at the end of this week. (they started planning for their wedding some time ago)
- He is / He's going to take the exam next year. (he is preparing for the exam now)

EXERCISE

Answer the questions.

1. What are you going to do this weekend?

2. Are you going to travel abroad next year?

3. When are you going to finish your project?

4. Who are you going to invite to your birthday party?

5. Why are you going to take a cooking class?

A1: *How much/many* and common uncountable nouns

How much and *How many* are used to ask about the quantity of something.

How much is used when referring to **uncountable nouns**, which are nouns that cannot be counted. They are always singular and do not have a plural form. Examples of uncountable nouns include: *water, milk, sugar, air, information, advice*, and *furniture*.

When asking about the quantity of uncountable nouns, we use *how much* followed by the uncountable noun.

Examples:

- **How much** <u>water</u> do you need?
- **How much** <u>sugar</u> do you want in your coffee?
- **How much** <u>air</u> is in the balloon?
- **How much** <u>information</u> do you have about this topic?

How many is used when referring to **countable nouns**, which are nouns that can be counted. They can be singular or plural (and usually add *s* or *es* in the plural form). Examples of countable nouns include: *book, pen, person, apple*, and *hour*.

When asking about the quantity of countable nouns, we use *how many* followed by the countable noun.

Examples:

- **How many** <u>books</u> do you have?
- **How many** <u>pens</u> do you need for the workshop?
- **How many** <u>apples</u> do you want?
- **How many** <u>hours</u> do you work in a month?
- **How many** <u>people</u> are in the room?

Some nouns can be both countable and uncountable depending on the context. For example, *water* is uncountable when referring to the substance, but countable when referring to cups of water.

Examples:

- **How much** <u>water</u> do you want? (uncountable)
- **How many** <u>cups of water</u> do you want? (countable)

You can make other uncountable nouns countable by adding what is called a "partitive" in front of them.

Examples:

- **a piece of** advice
- **a slice of** bread
- **a loaf of** bread
- **a tube of** toothpaste

EXERCISE

Are the nouns in this sentence countable (C) or uncountable (U)? How do you know?

1. How much milk do we need for the recipe?

2. How many apples are in the basket?

3. How much money did you spend on groceries?

4. How many books did you read last month?

5. How much sugar do you put in your coffee?

Answers: 1. U; 2. C; 3. U; 4. C; 5. U

A1: *I'd like*

The phrase *I'd like* (= *I would like*) is used to make a request or express a preference. It is more polite than *I want*.

Examples:

- I**'d like** a cup of coffee, please.
  (more polite than: I want a cup of coffee, please.)
- I**'d like** to sit by the window, if that's okay.
  (more polite than: I want to sit by the window.)
- He**'d like** to speak to the manager.
  (more polite than: He wants to speak to the manager.)
- **Would** you **like** an aisle seat or a window seat?
- (more polite than: Do you want an aisle seat or a window seat?)

It can also be used to express a wish.

Examples:

- I**'d like** to be a teacher.
- (If she had a million dollars) she**'d like** to travel the world.

EXERCISE

What are some things you'd like?

A1: Imperatives

An imperative is a form of a verb that is used to give commands or make requests. It is formed by using the base form of the verb (the infinitive without *to*) and is often used in the second person (you), but it can also be used in the first person (*let's*) or the third person (*let him, let them*) to give commands or advice.

Examples:

- **Close** the door. (second person)
- **Let's** go. (first person)
- **Let** him do it. (third person)

Imperatives can also be used to make polite requests. This is done by using *please, could,* or *can* before the imperative form of the verb.

Examples:

- Please **close** the door.
- Could you **pass** the salt (, please)?
- Can you **help** me with this (, please)?

Imperatives can be used to give negative commands as well by using *don't* before the imperative form of the verb.

Examples:

- Don't **touch** that!
- Don't **be** late!

An imperative can also be polite, rude, or forceful, depending on the speaker's tone of voice and the situation.

Instructions for tasks, such as making a recipe, often use imperatives. Imperatives help keep the information short.

Example:

- **Preheat** your oven to 350°F (175°C).
- **Grease** and **flour** two 9-inch round cake pans.
- In a large mixing bowl, **combine** the flour, sugar, baking soda, baking powder, and salt. **Whisk** together until evenly mixed.
- **Add** the eggs, buttermilk, hot water, and vegetable oil.
- **Mix** everything together.
- **Pour** the batter into the cake pans.
- **Bake** the cakes for 30–35 minutes.
- Once done, **remove** the cakes from the oven and **allow** them to cool.
- Carefully **remove** the cakes from the pans and **place** them on a wire rack to cool.
- **Decorate** the cake as desired.
- **Enjoy** your delicious cake!

EXERCISE

Complete the sentences with an appropriate imperative verb.

1. _____ the door, please. It's cold outside.

2. _____ your homework before watching TV.

3. _____ your seatbelt when you get in the car.

4. _____ the window, it's stuffy in here.

5. _____ me a favor and pass the salt, please.

Answers: 1. Close/Shut; 2. Do/Finish; 3. Fasten/Put on; 4. Open; 5. Do

A1: Intensifiers

Intensifiers are words or phrases that are used to add emphasis or intensity to a verb, adjective, or adverb.

- He's happy.
- He's **very** happy.
- He's **extremely** happy.

Some examples of intensifiers that can be used with **adjectives**:

- very (e.g., very happy, very cold)
- extremely (e.g., extremely happy, extremely cold)
- incredibly (e.g., incredibly happy, incredibly cold)
- totally (e.g., totally happy, totally cold)

Some examples of intensifiers that can be used with **adverbs**:

- really (He runs really fast.)
- quite (She sings quite well.)
- completely (He is completely exhausted.)

EXERCISE

Underline the intensifiers in the passage.

I am extremely tired after running in the hot weather today. It was utterly exhausting, and I am completely drained. The pizza I had for lunch was very delicious, but the dessert was quite sweet, and I couldn't eat it all. The traffic on the way back was really terrible, and I was incredibly bored listening to the same songs on the radio. Well, it was a totally exhausting day, but I am happy that I accomplished my running goal.

Answers: extremely, utterly, completely, very, quite, really, incredibly, totally

A1: Modals: *can, can't, could, couldn't*

Can, can't, could, and *couldn't* are all modal verbs that indicate the ability or possibility of something happening.

Can is used to indicate that something is possible or that someone has the ability to do something.

Examples:

- I **can** speak French. (indicates the ability to speak French)
- **Can** you help me with this? (indicates a possibility of someone helping)

Can't is the negative form of *can* and is used to indicate that something is not possible or that someone does not have the ability to do something.

Examples:

- I **can't** speak French. (indicates the inability to speak French)
- He **can't** come to the meeting. (indicates that it is not possible for him to come to the meeting)

Could is the past form of *can* and is used to indicate that something was possible or that someone had the ability to do something in the past.

Examples:

- I **could** speak French when I was a child. (indicates a past ability to speak French)
- **Could** you help me with this yesterday? (indicates a past possibility of someone helping)

Couldn't is the negative form of *could* and is used to indicate that something was not possible or that someone did not have the ability to do something in the past.

Examples:

- I **couldn't** speak French when I was a child. (indicates the past inability to speak French)
- He **couldn't** come to the meeting yesterday. (it was not possible for him to come to the meeting in the past)

Can is more informal than *could* and is often used in casual speech, while *could* is more formal and is often used in writing and more formal speaking situations.

EXERCISE

Choose the appropriate modal verb to complete the sentences.

1. I _____ swim when I was younger, but I can't swim now.

2. She _____ play the guitar, but she can't play it well.

3. They _____ speak French fluently, but they can't speak it perfectly.

4. You _____ go to the party if you want to.

5. I _____ finish this project on time if I work hard enough.

6. We _____ understand the instructions, because they were unclear.

7. She _____ believe what he said, but she didn't trust him.

Answers: 1. could; 2. can; 3. can; 4. can; 5. can; 6. couldn't; 7. could

A1: Past simple (Simple past) (basic)

(See also the A2 entry for Simple past)

The past simple (also known as the simple past or *preterite*), is a verb tense used to indicate that an action or state took place in the past and is now completed. It is formed by adding -*ed* to regular verbs (e.g., walk → walked, talk → talked). Irregular verbs take different forms in the past simple, and need to be learned separately (e.g., go → went, do → did, have → had).

Examples:

- I **walked** to the store.
- He **talked** to his friend.
- She **sang** a song.
- It **rained** yesterday.
- You **played** the guitar.
- We **traveled** to Japan.
- They **ate** dinner.

The past simple is often used in conjunction with time expressions such as *yesterday, last week, in 1995*, etc.

The past simple is different from the present perfect, which is used to talk about an action that occurred in the past but has relevance to the present. An example of this would be "I have seen that movie" instead of "I saw that movie."

Underline examples of the past simple in the passage.

Last weekend, I visited my grandparents who live in the countryside. We had a great time talking about the past. My grandfather told me about the time when he traveled to Europe by boat in the 1970s. He said it was an amazing experience, and he met many interesting people on the ship. My grandmother showed me a photo album of their wedding day. She looked beautiful in her white wedding dress, and my grandfather looked handsome in his suit. They married in the summer of 1979 in a small church in the town where they grew up. We also talked about their children—my mother and her two older sisters—and how they spent their summers playing outside in the fields and swimming in the nearby river. They spoke about the time when they had a farm and how they woke up early to feed the animals. They said it was hard work, but it was also rewarding. It was nice to hear these stories and learn about my family history. I hope to visit them again soon.

Answers: visited, had, told, traveled, said, was, met, showed, looked (x2), married, grew (up), talked, spent, spoke, had, woke (up), said, was (x3)

A1: Past simple of *to be*

The past simple of the verb *be* is **was** for the first and third person singular (*I*, *he*, *she*, *it*) and **were** for the second person singular and plural (*you*, *we*, *they*).

- I **was** tired yesterday.
- He **was** at the store.
- She **was** happy
- It **was** cold outside.
- You **were** right.
- We **were** at the beach.
- They **were** late.
- **Were** they late? They **weren't** late.
- **Were** you late? I **wasn't** late.
- **Was** he late? He **wasn't** late.

EXERCISE

Complete the sentences with the appropriate form of *be*.

1. She _____ happy to see her old friends.

2. They _____ at the party last night.

3. I _____ sure if I wanted to go out or stay home.

4. We _____ late for the meeting this morning.

5. The food at the restaurant _____ extremely delicious.

6. He _____ very good at playing the guitar.

7. You _____ at home when I called you.

8. _____ the weather nice today?

Answers: 1. was/wasn't; 2. were/weren't; 3. wasn't; 4. were/weren't; 5. was/wasn't; 6. was/wasn't; 7. were/weren't; 8. Was/Wasn't

A1: Possessive adjectives

Possessive adjectives are a type of adjective that indicate possession or ownership of something. They are used before a noun to show that the noun belongs to a specific person or thing. Possessive adjectives include:

- my (possession by the speaker)
- your (possession by the person being spoken to)
- his (possession by a boy/man)
- her (possession by a girl/woman)
- its (possession by an inanimate object or animal)
- our (possession by the speaker and one or more others)
- their (possession by a group of people or things)

Examples:

- **My** book is on the table. (the book belongs to the speaker)
- **Your** car is very nice. (the car belongs to the person being spoken to)
- **His** dog is very friendly. (the dog belongs to a male)
- **Her** dress is very pretty. (the dress belongs to a female)
- **Its** tail is very fluffy. (the tail belongs to an inanimate object or animal)
- **Our** project is due tomorrow. (the project belongs to the speaker and one or more others)
- **Their** house is very big. (the house belongs to a group of people or things)

Possessive adjectives always come before the noun they modify, they don't have plural forms, and they don't take an -s like in possessive pronouns.

Their can also refer to singular *he* or *she*.

Complete the sentences with a suitable possessive adjective.

1. _____ cat is sleeping on the sofa.

2. _____ brother is studying medicine at university.

3. _____ sister is a talented artist.

4. _____ dog loves to play fetch with a ball.

5. _____ parents have been married for 25 years.

6. _____ favorite color is blue.

7. _____ school is near the park.

8. _____ car is parked in the driveway.

9. _____ friends are coming over for dinner tonight.

10. _____ phone is ringing. Can you answer it?

A1: Possessive 's

The possessive 's is used to indicate possession or ownership of something. It is formed by adding -'s to the end of a noun, or just an apostrophe (') if the noun is already plural.

Examples:

- The dog**'s** tail wagged happily.
  (the tail belongs to the dog)
- The children**'s** toys were scattered on the floor.
  (the toys belong to the children)
- The company**'s** profits have increased.
  (the profits belong to the company)

When the noun is plural and already ends in -s, you only add an apostrophe **after** the noun to indicate possession.

Examples:

- the countrie**s'** wealth (= the wealth of the countries)
- the bosse**s'** decision (= the decision of the bosses)

In a name that ends in s, some writers will put an apostrophe after the noun ending in s, but some will add an apostrophe and s.

Examples:

- The Jones's house is very big. OR The Jones' house is very big.
- James's toys are everywhere. OR James' toys are everywhere.

It's important to differentiate between the possessive 's and the contraction of *is*, which is also written as 's. For example: The boy's hat (possessive – the hat belongs to the boy) vs The boy's playing (contraction of *The boy is playing*).

A1: Prepositions

Prepositions are words that indicate the relationship of a noun or pronoun to other words in a sentence. They often indicate the location, direction, or time of an action or event. The most common prepositions are:

- in (location or time within a certain place or period)
- on (location on a surface or a specific time)
- at (a specific location or time)
- with (the person/thing accompanying another person/thing)
- to (direction or destination)
- from (the starting point of an action or movement)
- of (possession or association)
- about (the subject or topic of something)
- like (similarity or preference)
- over (position above something)
- under (position below something)
- above (position higher than something)
- below (position lower than something)
- behind (position at the back of something)
- in front of (position at the front of something)
- beside (position next to something)
- between (position between two things)
- through (movement from one side to the other)

Example sentences:

- He is **at** the store. (indicates the specific location)
- I am going **to** the beach with my friends. (indicates the person moving to a place)
- She is **from** France. (indicates her origin)
- The Statue of Liberty is **in** New York. (indicates the location of the statue)

Some prepositions, such as *by* and *for*, can have different meanings depending on the context of the sentence.

Examples:

- It's **by** the door. (next to)
- The painting is **by** Picasso. (made by someone)
- I walked **for** miles. (an amount of distance)
- This flower is **for** you. (intended to be given to)

EXERCISE

Complete the sentences with a suitable preposition.

1. The book is _____ the desk.

2. We went for a walk _____ the park.

3. The restaurant is _____ the corner of the street.

4. She arrived _____ the airport early in the morning.

5. The cat is hiding _____ the couch.

6. He lives _____ a big house on the hill.

7. The movie starts _____ 7 PM at the theater.

8. The coffee shop is _____ the street from the library.

9. She's been working _____ the company for five years.

10. They traveled _____ Europe for three months last summer.

Answers: 1. on; 2. in; 3. on; 4. at; 5. under; 6. in; 7. at; 8. across; 9. at; 10. around/throughout

A1: Prepositions of time (*in, on, at*)

Prepositions of time indicate when an event or action occurs. They describe the relationship between the time of an event and the time of reference. Some common prepositions of time include:

- in (used for a period of time, such as months, years, centuries, or seasons)
- at (used for specific times or points in time, such as clock times or holidays)
- on (used for specific days or dates)

Examples:

- I'll see you **in** three days. (indicates a period of time in the future)
- The store closes **at** 9 PM. (indicates a specific time)
- We're going to the coast **on** Monday. (indicates a specific day)
- I'll see you **in** the morning. (indicates a time of day)
- The weather is hot **in** (the) summer. (indicates a season)

EXERCISE

Choose the correct time preposition.

1. I usually wake up **in / at / on** 6:30 during the week.

2. My birthday is **in / at / on** September.

3. Their wedding is **in / at / on** 12th April.

4. I have a meeting **in / at / on** the afternoon.

5. The train arrives **in / at / on** midnight.

Answers: 1. at; 2. in; 3. on; 4. in; 5. at

A1: Present simple (Simple present)

The present simple is a verb tense formed by using the base form of the verb (the infinitive without *to*). There are three main uses of the present simple.

1. to describe actions or states that are regularly (habitually) true

Examples:

- I **eat** breakfast every morning. (a regular action)
- They **play** soccer every Saturday. (a regular action)
- He **studies** for his exams every night. (a regular action)

2. to describe a general truth or fact

Examples:

- The Earth **goes** around the Sun.
- Cats **have** fur.
- Everyone **ages**.
- Water **boils** at 100 degrees Celsius.
- There **are** 100 centimeters in a meter.

3. to describe future actions or events that have been planned or scheduled

Examples:

- The train **leaves** at 5 PM.
- My flight **arrives** tomorrow at 8 AM.

A1: Present continuous

The present continuous can be used to talk about:

- temporary actions or events that are happening right now
- actions that have already started and will continue in the near future
- actions or events with a strong connection to the present

It is formed by combining the present form of the verb *to be* (*am*, *is*, or *are*) with the present participle (*-ing*) form of the main verb.

Examples:

- I **am eating** breakfast. (the action of eating breakfast is currently happening)
- I **am reading** a book. (the action of reading has already started and will continue)
- They **are working** at the bank. (the action of working has a connection to the present)

The present continuous can also be used to talk about future plans or arrangements that have been made.

Examples:

- I**'m meeting** my friend later. (the action of meeting has been arranged for a specific time in the future)
- We**'re going** to the movies tonight. (the action of going to the movies has been planned for a specific time in the future)

The present continuous is not used to describe actions or events that are permanent or unchanging.

Question forms begin with *Is/Are* or *Do*.

Examples:

- **Are** you **enjoying** your salad?
- **Do** you like **studying**?

Negative forms use *not*.

Examples:

- I am not having fun.
- She is not doing her homework.
- They aren't (are not) going there.

EXERCISES

---

1. Write five sentences to say what you are doing now or are planning to do in the near future.

1.

2.

3.

4.

5.

2. Read the passage and answer the questions using the present simple tense.

My name is Sarah and I am a teacher. I work in a school in the city. I teach music to students from all over the world. My classes start at 9 AM and finish at 3 PM In the morning, I usually have three lessons, and in the afternoon, I have two. My students are very friendly and always eager to learn.

1. What is the name of the person speaking?

2. What does Sarah do?

3. Where does Sarah work?

4. What does Sarah teach?

5. What time do Sarah's classes start and finish?

6. How many lessons does Sarah have in the morning and how many in the afternoon?

7. Are Sarah's students friendly?

8. Do Sarah's students want to learn?

Answers: 1. Her name is Sarah; 2. Sarah is a teacher; 3. Sarah works in a school in the city; 4. Sarah teaches music; 5. Sarah's classes start at 9 AM and finish at 3 PM; 6. Sarah has three lessons in the morning and two in the afternoon; 7. Yes, Sarah's students are friendly; 8. Yes, Sarah's students want to learn.

A1: Pronouns: personal

Personal pronouns include *I, me, you, he, him, she, her, it, we, us, they, them.*

Personal pronouns are divided into **subject pronouns** (*I, you [singular], he, she, it, we, you [plural], they*) and **object pronouns** (*me, you [singular], her, him, them, us, you [plural] them*).

Examples of subject pronouns:

- **He** went to the store. (the subject is a man)
- **She** is my friend. (the subject is a woman)
- **They** are my friends. (the subject is a group of more than one person)

Examples of object pronouns:

- He gave it to **me**. (I am the object of the sentence)
- We came to see **you**. (you are the object of the sentence)

Pronouns can substitute nouns in a sentence. This avoids repetition. They can be the subject or the object of a sentence.

Examples:

- I have a <u>cat</u>. **Her** name is Farah.
- I have a <u>cat</u>. Farah is **her** name.
- I have a <u>cat</u>. Farah is the name of **her**.

Pronouns also have possessive, and reflexive forms[3].

Examples:

- That book is **mine**. (possessive pronoun)
- I did it **myself**. (reflexive pronoun)

---

[3] See the back of the book for lists of all English pronouns

Complete the sentences with a correct personal pronoun.

1. _____ am going to the store.

2. _____ are going to the store.

3. _____ is going to the store.

4. _____ are going to the store.

5. _____ is my sister.

6. _____ is my brother.

7. _____ is my cat.

8. _____ are my parents.

9. The book is on the table. _____ is a good book.

10. The books are on the table. _____ are good books.

Answers: 1. am; 2. You/We; 3. He/She; 4. You/We; 5. She; 6. He; 7. It; 8. They; 9. It; 10. They

A1: *Some* and *any*

We use *some* and *any* with plural nouns and countable nouns.

Some is used in positive sentences.

Examples:

- I have some information for you. (information = uncountable)
- I met some friends in town. (friends = countable, plural)
- I met a friend in town. (friend = countable, singular)

Any is used in negative sentences to mean "none at all."

Examples:

- I don't have any water. (water = uncountable)
- I didn't give him any advice. (advice = uncountable)
- Don't give him any advice!

Any or *some* can be used in questions.

We use *any* when we really don't know what the answer is.

Example:

- Can you see any birds? (birds = countable, plural)

Some is used when we are:

- asking for something: Can I have some paper, please?
- offering something: Would you like some tea?
- suggesting something: Why don't you do some yoga?

EXERCISE

Say what you have and don't have in your fridge or cupboard.

A1: Questions

In English, there are several ways to form a question.

Yes/No questions: These are questions that can be answered with *yes* or *no*. They are formed by using the auxiliary (helping) verb *do* or *does* followed by the subject and the verb base form.

Examples:

- Do you like pizza?
- Does he play guitar?

Wh- questions: These are questions that begin with a *wh-* word: *what, when, where, who, whom, which, whose,* and *why.*

Examples:

- What do you want to eat?
- Where do you live?
- Who is your favorite actor?

Tag questions: These are questions that are formed by adding a small tag at the end of a statement. The tag is usually the auxiliary verb *do* or *does* followed by the pronoun.

Examples:

- You're from Canada, aren't you?
- He can speak Spanish, can't he?

Alternative questions: These are questions that are formed by adding *or* between two options.

Examples:

- Would you like coffee or tea?
- Do you prefer hot or cold weather?

Embedded questions: These are questions that are embedded in a sentence, usually after a phrase like "I wonder" or "Do you know." The word order can change.

Examples:

- I wonder what the time is.
- Do you know where my keys are?

Complete the sentences by forming a question.

1. She likes pizza. (*Yes/No* question) → *Does she ... ?*

2. He is reading a book. (*Wh-* question)

3. You aren't coming to the party, _____? (tag question)

4. She is a doctor or a nurse, isn't she? (alternative question)

5. They watched a movie last night. (*Wh-* question)

6. He doesn't like coffee, _____? (tag question)

7. We can go to the beach or the pool, can't we? (alternative question)

8. You have a dog, _____? (*Yes/No* question)

9. She is going to the store. (*Wh-* question)

10. They don't speak Spanish, _____? (tag question)

Answers: 1. Does she like pizza?; 2. What is he reading?; 3. aren't you; 4. Is she a doctor or a nurse?; 5. What did they watch/do last night? 6. does he; 7. Can we go to the beach or the pool? 8. don't you; 9. Where is she going?; 10. do they

A1: *There is/are*

There is and *there are* are used to indicate the presence of something or someone in a particular place.

There is is used to indicate that there is one thing or person in a particular place. It is formed by using the word *there* followed by the verb *to be* in the present tense (*is*) and a singular noun.

Examples:

- **There is** a book on the table.
- **There is** a man at the door.

There are is used to indicate that there are multiple things or people in a particular place. It is formed by using the word *there* followed by the verb *to be* in the present tense (*are*) and a plural noun.

Examples:

- **There are** three apples in the basket.
- **There are** many people in the park.

The question forms reverse the order of the words.

Examples:

- **Are there** three apples in the basket?
- **Are there** many people in the park?
- **Is there** any ice in the fridge?

Say what is in the room. Use *there is* and *there are*.

A1: *To be*

The verb *to be* is perhaps the most used English verb. It is used to indicate the existence or presence of something or someone. It is also used to indicate identity, characteristics, and location. In the present tense, the verb *to be* has two forms: *am* and *are* (1st and 2nd person singular and plural), and *is* (3rd person singular).

Examples:

- I **am** a student.
- You **are** my friend.
- He **is** tall.
- We **are** happy.
- They **are** here.

The negative form of the present tense of the verb *to be* is formed by adding *not* after the verb.

Examples:

- I **am** not a student.
- You **are** not my friend.
- He **is** not tall.
- We **are** not happy.
- They **are** not here.

To form a question in the present tense, the word order is changed to subject-verb-object.

Examples:

- **Am** I a student?
- **Are** you my friend?
- **Is** he tall?
- **Are** we happy?
- **Are** they here?

The past tense of the verb *to be* is *was* for singular subjects and *were* for plural subjects.

Examples:

- I **was** a student.
- You **were** my friend.
- He **was** tall.
- We **were** happy.
- They **were** here.

The negative form of the past tense of the verb *to be* is formed by adding *not* after the verb.

Examples:

- I **was** not a student.
- You **were** not my friend.
- He **was** not tall.
- We **were** not happy.
- They **were** not here.

To form a question in the past tense, the word order is changed to subject-verb-object.

Examples:

- **Was** I a student?
- **Were** you my friend?
- **Was** he tall?
- **Were** we happy?
- **Were** they here?

To be is also used in a variety of idiomatic expressions and can be used as an auxiliary verb to form the passive.

A1: Verb + -*ing*: *like, hate, love*

(See also the A2 entry for Verb + -ing/infinitive*)*

Certain verbs, such as *like*, *hate*, and *love* are linking verbs, which means that they connect the subject of the sentence to a noun or adjective. These verbs are often followed by present participles (verb forms with -*ing*).

Examples:

- I **like** play**ing** basketball.
- She **hates** eat**ing** broccoli.
- They **love** danc**ing**.

Whether you use the -*ing* form or *to* + infinitive depends on the context and the meaning you want to convey. For example, "I like to play basketball" indicates that playing basketball is something that you enjoy doing, while "I like playing basketball" can indicate that you are in the process of playing basketball.

EXERCISE

Say what you like, hate, and love doing.

A2: Adverbial phrases of time, place and frequency – including word order

Adverbial phrases of time, place, and frequency are groups of words that function as adverbs and give additional information about an action. They are used to answer questions like *when? where?* and *how often?*

Adverbial phrases of time include words like *yesterday*, *last week*, *at 5 PM*, and *in the morning*. These phrases give information about when the action takes place.

Adverbial phrases of place include words like *at home*, *in the park*, and *on the bus*. These phrases give information about where the action takes place.

Adverbial phrases of frequency include words like *always*, *never*, *sometimes*, and *once a week*. These phrases give information about how often the action takes place.

In terms of word order, adverbial phrases of time, place, and frequency are usually placed after the main verb or after the subject in a sentence.

Examples:

- I'll meet you **at the park** later. (adverbial phrase of place)
- She goes to the gym **every day**. (adverbial phrase of frequency)

The word order can vary depending on the sentence structure and the emphasis that the speaker wants to give. However, the basic word order of adverbial phrases is usually *after* the main verb or the subject.

A2: Adverbs of frequency

Adverbs of frequency are words that describe how often an action takes place. They are used to answer the question *how often?* Adverbs of frequency can be placed before the main verb or after the verb *to be*. Some common adverbs of frequency are *always*, *usually*, *often*, *sometimes*, *occasionally*, *rarely*, and *never*.

Examples:

- I **always** eat breakfast at 7 AM. (before the main verb)
- She is **usually** very busy in the morning. (after the verb *to be*)

The position of adverbs of frequency can affect the meaning of a sentence. When an adverb of frequency is placed before the main verb, it has a stronger emphasis on the frequency of the action. When it's placed after the verb *to be*, it has a weaker emphasis and focuses more on the state or condition of the subject.

Additionally, there are specific rules for ordering multiple adverbs of frequency in a sentence. For example, when a sentence contains an adverb of frequency and an adverb of manner (such as *quickly*), the adverb of frequency usually comes first.

Example:

- She **often quickly** finishes her work. (adverb of frequency first)

A2: Articles

Articles are words that are used before nouns to indicate the noun's grammatical definiteness. In English, there are two types of articles: definite articles and indefinite articles.

The **definite article** *the* is used before a specific noun that the listener or reader knows about, or has already been mentioned.

Example:

- The book on **the** table is mine.

The **indefinite articles** *a* and *an* are used before a non-specific noun that the listener or reader does not know about, or has not been mentioned. *A* is used before a noun that starts with a consonant sound, and *an* is used before a noun that starts with a vowel sound.

Examples:

- **A** book is lying on the floor. (one book; we don't know this book – it is the first time it is mentioned)
- **An** apple is a type of fruit. (one apple – an unspecific noun; we could also say here "Apples are a type of fruit.")

A and *an* cannot be used with uncountable nouns or plural nouns.

Examples:

- **The** ice is melting. (*ice* is an uncountable noun)
- **The** books are on the shelf. (*books* is a plural noun)

Complete the sentences by choosing the correct definite or indefinite article.

1. **A / The** English teacher gave us an assignment.

2. **An / The** apple a day keeps the doctor away.

3. I need **a / the** book on history for my research.

4. **A / The** lion is the king of the jungle.

5. She is **a / an** actress in Hollywood.

6. **The / An** African elephant has the largest ears.

7. He has **a / the** passion for music.

8. **A / The** sun sets in the west.

9. I need **a / the** pen to write this letter.

10. **The / An** oak tree needs to be cut down.

Answers: 1. A; 2. An; 3. a; 4. A; 5. an; 6. The; 7. a; 8. The; 9. a; 10. The

A2: Comparatives: use of *than* and *the*

(See also the A1 entry for Comparatives and superlatives)

When comparing two things, the definite article *the* should be used before the second item being compared:

- She is **taller** <u>than</u> <u>the</u> other girls.
- This car is **faster** <u>than</u> <u>the</u> one we saw yesterday.

EXERCISE

Complete the sentences by adding the correct form of the comparative adjective in parentheses[4].

1. This book is (interesting) than the one I read last week.

2. That car is (expensive) than my car.

3. Mary is (smart) than her classmates.

4. The weather today is (good) than yesterday.

5. The red dress is (pretty) than the blue one.

6. This exercise is (easy) than the previous one.

7. The food here is (delicious) than the food there.

8. Lara's English is (fluent) than it was last year.

9. The coffee at this café is (strong) than the coffee at the other café.

10. John's grades are (good) than his brother's grades.

Answers: 1. more interesting; 2. more expensive; 3. smarter; 4. better; 5. prettier; 6. easier; 7. more delicious; 8. more fluent; 9. stronger; 10. better

---

[4] parentheses = *(* and *)* [some people call these "brackets"]

A2: Conditionals: zero and first

The zero conditional and the first conditional are two forms of conditional sentences in English grammar.

The **zero conditional** is used to express a general truth, a scientific fact, or a habit. The structure of a zero conditional sentence is: *if* + present simple, present simple.

Examples:

- **If** you **heat** water to 100 degrees Celsius, it **boils**. (a scientific fact)
- **If** you **water** plants, they **grow**. (a habit)

The **first conditional** is used to express a possible future situation based on a present condition. The structure of a first conditional sentence is *if* + present simple, *will* + infinitive.

Examples:

- **If** it **rains**, I will stay at home. (the speaker believes that there is a chance of rain and that they will stay at home if it does rain)
- **If** she **passes** the test, she will be very happy. (the speaker believes that there is a chance she will pass the test and will be happy if she does)

The first conditional refers to a specific future event that is likely to happen if a certain condition is met, whereas the zero conditional refers to a general truth that always holds true, regardless of any particular condition.

Rewrite the sentences using the zero conditional and the first conditional.

1. If you eat too much, you get a stomachache.

Zero conditional: You _____.

First conditional: If you _____.

2. If I miss the bus, I'll be late for class.

Zero conditional: First conditional:

3. If she studies hard, she'll pass the exam.

Zero conditional: First conditional:

4. If they don't hurry, they'll miss the movie.

Zero conditional: First conditional:

5. If you press the button, the machine starts.

Zero conditional: First conditional:

Answers: 1. Zero: You get a stomachache if you eat too much. First: If you eat too much, you will get a stomachache.; 2. Zero: I'll be late for class if I miss the bus. First: If I miss the bus, I will be late for class.; 3. Zero: She passes the exam if she studies hard. First: If she studies hard, she will pass the exam.; 4. Zero: They miss the movie if they don't hurry. First: If they don't hurry, they will miss the movie.; 5. Zero: The machine starts if you press the button. First: If you press the button, the machine will start.

A2: Countable and uncountable nouns with *much/many*

Much and *many* are used to express the quantity of countable and uncountable nouns.

Countable nouns are nouns that can be counted, such as *book, person, dog*. When expressing the quantity of countable nouns, we use ***many***.

Examples:

- I have **many** books.
- There are **many** people in the room.

Uncountable nouns are nouns that cannot be counted, such as *water, music, air*. When expressing the quantity of uncountable nouns, we use ***much***.

Examples:

- I have much water. (the same as: I have a lot of water.)
- There is not much music in the playlist. (the same as: *There is not a lot of music in the playlist.*)

A2: Future time (*will* and *going to*)

(See also the A1 entry for Going to *and the B1 entry* Will and going to – for prediction)

In English, there are two main ways to talk about future events or actions: using *will* or *going to*.

Will is used to express a simple prediction or a spontaneous decision made at the time of speaking.

Examples:

- I **will** meet you at the station. (Depending on the context, this can mean that the speaker suddenly decides to meet the person at the station, or that the speaker is predicting/guessing that they will meet the other person at the station – they might not meet at the station, instead they might meet at another place.)
- He **will** come with us to the party.

Going to is used to describe a future event or action that has already been planned or arranged:

Examples:

- We are **going to** have a picnic this weekend.
- I'm **going to** study for my exam tomorrow.

Both *will* and *going to* can also be used in questions to ask about future plans or arrangements:

Examples:

- Are you **going to** visit your grandparents this weekend?
- **Will** you help me with the move on Saturday?

Will and *going to* also have other uses and meanings in English, such as in making requests, offering help, or expressing willingness.

Also, speakers sometimes use *will* and *going to* interchangeably, regardless of the "rules" about when each one should be used.

EXERCISE

Complete the sentences with either *will* or *going to*.

1. The weather forecast said it _____ rain today.

2. I'm not sure what I'm going to wear to the party. I _____ decide later.

3. She _____ start a new job next week.

4. I'm so tired. I _____ go to bed early tonight.

5. They _____ take a trip to Europe next summer.

6. The concert _____ start in five minutes.

7. I _____ visit my grandparents tomorrow.

8. I'm sorry, I can't come to the party on Monday. I _____ be out of town.

9. They _____ have a baby in the next few months.

10. I'm not sure what to do about the problem. I _____ think about it for a while.

Answers: 1. is going to/will; 2. will; 3. is going to; 4. am going to; 5. are going to; 6. will; 7. am going to; 8. will; 9. are going to; 10. will

A2: Gerunds

A gerund is a verb form that ends in *-ing* and functions as a noun in a sentence. A gerund can be used as a subject, an object, or a complement, and can take on the roles of a noun, such as being the object of a preposition.

Examples:

- **Swimming** is my favorite sport. (subject of the sentence)
- I enjoy reading books. (object of the sentence)
- His hobby is **playing the guitar**. (complement of the sentence)
- I'm tired of **listening to the same music over and over**. (object of the preposition "of")

A gerund can also be used as a modifier, such as in a gerund phrase, which is a phrase that includes a gerund and any related objects or modifiers.

Examples:

- The man **eating a sandwich** is my friend.
- **Running in the park** is a good way to start the day.

Complete the sentences with a suitable gerund. Then identify if each gerund is being used as a subject, an object, or a complement.

1. _____ is my favorite summer activity.

2. I love _____ delicious meals for my friends.

3. My main goal is _____ my degree in four years.

4. _____ is good for your health.

5. I enjoy _____ to music while studying.

6. His passion is _____ the piano.

7. My favorite hobby is _____ science fiction novels.

8. They are considering _____ their house.

9. The best way to learn a new language is _____ with locals when traveling overseas.

10. She always avoids _____ her homework until the last minute.

Possible answers: 1. swimming (subject); 2. cooking (object); 3. finishing (complement); 4. running (subject); 5. listening (object); 6. playing (complement); 7. reading (complement); 8. renovating (object); 9. speaking (subject); 10. doing (object)

A2: Modals: *have to*

The modal verb *have to* is used to express obligation, necessity, or requirement in English.

Examples:

- I **have to** go to work every day.
- She **has to** finish her homework before dinner.
- We **don't have to** attend the meeting tomorrow.

Have to is different from other modal verbs in that it can also be used to express external obligation, meaning that the obligation comes from outside the speaker, rather than from the speaker's own beliefs or feelings.

Examples:

- I **have to** pay my taxes.
- Students **have to** take an exam at the end of the course.

Have to can be contracted to *has to* or *had to*, depending on the subject and tense used in the sentence. Additionally, the negative form of *have to* is *don't have to* or *doesn't have to*.

Complete the sentences by adding the correct form of *have to*.

1. She _____ finish her project by next Friday.

2. They _____ attend the meeting at 10 AM earlier today.

3. He _____ take the bus to work, because his car was in the shop.

4. We _____ wear uniforms at our school.

5. You _____ be at the airport two hours before your flight.

6. They _____ pay the bills every month.

7. She _____ go to the dentist next week.

8. He _____ get up early to catch the train.

9. We _____ follow the rules of the road when we drive.

10. You _____ book your hotel in advance for your trip.

Answers: 1. has to; 2. had to; 3. had to; 4. have to; 5. have to / had to; 6. have to / had to; 7. has to; 8. has to / had to; 9. have to; 10. have to / had to

A2: Modals: *should*

The modal verb *should* is used to give advice, recommendations, or suggestions in English. It can also be used to express expectation, duty, or moral obligation.

Examples:

- You **should** take an umbrella with you, it might rain.
- She **should** eat more vegetables.
- We **should** be polite to everyone.

Should can also be used to express probability or expectation in the present or future, based on what is considered likely/typical.

Examples:

- The train **should** arrive at 10:30.
- They **should** be home by now.

In the negative form, *should* becomes *shouldn't*.

Examples:

- You **shouldn't** smoke, it's bad for your health.
- They **shouldn't** be late for the meeting.

In questions, *should* comes at the beginning.

Example:

- **Should** we go before or after dinner?

In its past form, *should have* contracts to *should've*.

A2: Past continuous (Past progressive)

The past continuous (also known as the past progressive) is a verb tense used to describe an action or event that was ongoing or in progress at a specific point in the past. It is formed by combining the auxiliary verb *was/were* with the present participle of the main verb, which ends in *-ing*.

Examples:

- Yesterday at 7 PM, I **was walking** in the park.
- They **were having** dinner when the phone rang.

The past continuous emphasizes the duration of the action and the fact that it was happening in the background while other actions or events were taking place. It is often used with the past simple tense to describe two actions happening at the same time in the past.

EXERCISE

Write five sentences that use the past continuous.

1.

2.

3.

4.

5.

A2: Past simple (Simple past)

(See also the A1 entry for Past simple)

The past simple (also known as the simple past) is a verb tense used to describe actions or events that have already happened and have no connection to the present. It is formed by adding *-ed* to regular verbs or by using a different form for irregular verbs.

Examples:

- Yesterday, I **walked** to the park. (walk → walked [regular])
- She **sang** a beautiful song last night. (sing → sang [irregular])

The past simple can be used to describe a single finished action in the past, a series of finished actions, or a habit or repeated action in the past. It is also used to describe past states or conditions.

To use the past simple in questions or in a negative sentence, you need the auxiliary verb *do*.

Examples:

- **Did** you **go** there?
- No, I **didn't go** there.

Note the common learner mistake made with the verb *born*. The dictionary form of this verb is *to be born*, and an example of a correct past simple sentence with this verb is:

- I was borned in Toronto in 1995.

EXERCISE

Write five sentences/questions that use the past simple.

A2: Phrasal verbs (common)

(See also the B1 entry for Phrasal verbs [advanced]*)*

Phrasal verbs are two- or three-word verbs that are made up of a base verb and one or two particles. They are common in everyday English (but not so common in formal writing) and often have a meaning that is different from the base verb on its own.

Here are some examples of common phrasal verbs:

- **Get up:** to rise from bed in the morning
- **Look after:** to take care of
- **Turn off:** to stop the operation of
- **Put on:** to dress oneself with
- **Take off:** to remove
- **Break down:** to stop functioning
- **Get away:** to escape or depart
- **Turn up:** to arrive unexpectedly

Phrasal verbs can be **separable** or **inseparable**. In separable phrasal verbs, the object can be placed between the verb and the particle, while in inseparable phrasal verbs, the object must be placed after the particle.

Examples:

- She put **on** her coat. (separable)
- She put her coat **on**. (inseparable)

A2: Prepositional phrases (place, time, and movement)

Prepositional phrases are groups of words that start with a preposition and end with a noun or pronoun. They can add information about place, time, and movement to sentences. It is a good idea to learn the group of words in the phrases together.

Prepositional phrases of **place** describe the location of something or someone.

Examples:

- I live **in a small town**.
- The cat is **on the couch**.
- We will meet **at the park**.

Prepositional phrases of **time** describe when something happened or will happen.

Examples:

- The party is **on Saturday**.
- I usually go to bed **in the evening**.
- The meeting is **at 3 PM**.

Prepositional phrases of **movement** describe the direction of an action.

Examples:

- She is walking **to the store**.
- The car drove **from the city to the countryside**.
- He jumped **into the pool**.

A2: Questions

In English grammar, questions are sentences that ask for information or clarification. They typically begin with a question word. The most common English question words are:

- **What**: used to ask for information about a thing or event
- **Where**: used to ask about a location or place
- **When**: used to ask about time
- **Why**: used to ask for a reason or explanation
- **Who**: used to ask about a person or people
- **Whom**: used to ask about the object of a sentence
- **Whose**: used to ask about possession
- **Which**: used to ask for a choice or decision
- **How**: used to ask about the method or manner
- **Whether**: used to ask about the possibility or existence of something. (Note that whether doesn't usually start a question.)

Example questions:

- What is your name?
- Where do you live?
- When did you arrive?
- Why did you leave early?
- Who is she?
- Whom are you speaking to?
- Whose book is this?
- Which movie do you want to see?
- How did you get here?
- Do you know whether it will rain tomorrow?

Read the passage and answer the questions.

As a child, Mari was fascinated with the stars. She spent hours at her bedroom window, gazing up at the night sky, trying to spot constellations and planets. Her parents recognized her love for astronomy and encouraged her to follow it. Mari's passion for the stars only grew stronger as she got older, and she decided to study astrophysics in college. Today, she is a successful astronomer who spends her nights observing the universe and discovering new galaxies.

1. What was Mari's childhood fascination?
2. Where did Mari spend a lot of time as a child?
3. Who encouraged Mari to pursue her passion for the stars?
4. When did Mari decide to study astrophysics in college?
5. Which college major did Mari choose to study?
6. How does Mari spend her nights now?

Answers: 1. the stars; 2. at her bedroom window; 3. her parents; 4. as she got older; 5. astrophysics; 6. observing the universe and discovering new galaxies

A2: Verb + *ing*/infinitive

(See also the A1 entry for Verb + -ing: like, hate, love*)*

The structure verb + *ing* or infinitive is used to express actions, activities, preferences, or states.

The verb + *ing* form (also known as the present participle) is used to describe an action that is happening now or in the present. Examples of verbs followed by the *-ing* form are *enjoy*, *hate*, and *love*:

- I **enjoy** listen**ing** to music.
- I **hate** wait**ing** in line.
- I **love** danc**ing**.

The infinitive form, which is usually preceded by the word *to*, is used to express a general action, rather than a specific, ongoing one. Examples of verbs followed by the infinitive form include *like*, *want*, and *would like*:

- I **like to read** books.
- I **want to learn** a new language.
- I **would like to travel** more.

In general, the choice between the verb + *ing* and infinitive form depends on the verb and the intended meaning. In the case of the verb like, it can be followed by the *-ing* present participle or the infinitive. In the following sentences, the meanings are the same.

- I **like to read**.
- I **like reading**.

A2: *Wh-* questions in past

Wh- questions in the past time are questions that ask about something that happened in the past. They are formed using the past simple tense, which is used to talk about completed actions or events in the past. Example questions using *wh-* words:

- **What** did you do yesterday?
- **When** did the train arrive?
- **Where** did you go on your last vacation?
- **Who** was the president in 1990?
- **Whom** did you meet last night?
- **Whose** book is this?
- **Which** movie did you see last week?
- **How** did you get here?

The verb in the question needs to be in the past simple tense, and if the verb is irregular, it must be used in its past simple irregular form.

Few people know how to use *whom* correctly, and often use *who* instead. *Whom* sounds very formal.

EXERCISE

Ask five *Wh-* questions about events or people in the past.

1.

2.

3.

4.

5.

B1: Adverbs

Adverbs are words that modify or describe verbs, adjectives, or other adverbs. They indicate the manner, time, place, degree, frequency, or certainty of the action or quality being described.

There are different types of adverbs, including:

- **Manner adverbs:** describe how an action is performed, such as *quickly* or *slowly*.
- **Time adverbs:** describe when an action occurs, such as *now* or *yesterday*.
- **Place adverbs:** describe where an action occurs, such as *here* or *there*.
- **Degree adverbs:** describe the extent or intensity of an action or quality, such as *very* or *completely*.
- **Frequency adverbs:** describe how often an action occurs, such as *always* or *never*.
- **Certainty adverbs:** describe the degree of certainty or possibility of an action or quality, such as *probably* or *surely*.

Adverbs can be placed at various positions in a sentence, depending on their meaning and purpose. For example, adverbs of frequency typically come before the main verb, while adverbs of manner often come after the main verb.

Examples:

- I eat **quickly**. (manner adverb)
- She visited her parents **yesterday**. (time adverb)
- They live **here**. (place adverb)
- She sings **very** well. (degree adverb)
- We **always** eat breakfast together. (frequency adverb)
- It will **probably** rain tomorrow. (certainty adverb)

B1: Broader range of intensifiers, including *too* and *enough*

Intensifiers are words or phrases that add emphasis to other words in a sentence. Some common intensifiers in English are:

Very: This is the most common intensifier and is used to describe something in a very strong or exaggerated way. Example: "She is very beautiful."

Really: This intensifier is used to express emphasis or surprise. Example: "I really enjoyed that movie."

Extremely: This intensifier is used to describe something in the strongest or most absolute terms. Example: "The weather is extremely cold today."

Absolutely: This intensifier is used to emphasize the speaker's agreement or conviction. Example: "I absolutely love that song."

Completely: This intensifier is used to describe something in the strongest or most absolute terms. Example: "I'm completely exhausted."

Too: Indicates that something is excessive or greater than what is desirable. Example: "The cake is too sweet."

Enough: Indicates that something is sufficient or satisfactory. Example: "This is enough food for everyone."

Intensifiers can also come in the form of adverbial phrases, such as *a lot* or *so much*. Example: I don't like that painting so much.

B1: Complex question tags

Complex question tags are used to turn a statement into a question or to confirm or challenge a speaker's understanding. They are typically formed by adding a tag question to the end of a sentence, starting with the auxiliary verb or a pronoun, followed by a subject pronoun.

Examples:

- She's leaving tomorrow, **isn't she**?
- You like cheese, **don't you**?

It's important to use the correct verb form in the question tag to match the tense of the main clause, and to use the right subject pronoun to match the subject of the main clause.

Examples:

- She**'s** leaving tomorrow, **isn't** she?
- She **isn't** leaving tomorrow, **is** she?

Question tags should be spoken with care to avoid sounding impolite, aggressive, or overly pushy. If we expect a listener to say "yes" to our question, the question tag should be spoken with falling intonation.

EXERCISE

Ask five questions that use question tags.

B1: Conditionals: second and third

The **second conditional** is a grammatical structure used to talk about hypothetical or unlikely events or situations in the present or future and their consequences. It is formed by combining the past simple form of the verb *to be* (*were*) with an infinitive verb. The structure of a second conditional sentence is as follows: *If* + subject + past simple verb, subject + *would* + infinitive verb.

Examples:

- **If** it **rains**, we <u>would stay</u> at home.
- **If** I **won** the lottery, I <u>would buy</u> a house.

In a second conditional sentence, the clause that starts with *if* states the hypothetical or unlikely condition, and the clause that starts with *would* states the consequence of that condition. The second conditional is used to express polite requests, suggestions, and desires.

The **third conditional** is a type of conditional sentence used to talk about past events that did not happen and their hypothetical consequences. It is formed using the conditional phrase *if* + past perfect verb tense, followed by *would have* + past participle[5].

Example:

- **If** he **had known** the answer, he <u>would have</u> answered the question.

In this example, the past perfect verb tense *had known* expresses the past event that did not happen, and the conditional phrase *would have answered* expresses the hypothetical consequence of that event. The third conditional is often used to express regret about a past event, or to make an imaginary change to the past.

---

[5] See the back of the book for a list of common past participles

B1: Connecting words (conjunctions)

Connecting words (also known as **conjunctions**) are words used to connect clauses, phrases, or sentences to express a relationship between them. They help to add extra information to a simple sentence.

The most basic connecting words are *and*, *or*, *but*, and *so*.

When these words connect two independent clauses (i.e., both clauses contain a subject and a verb), a comma is used.

Example:

- I like movies, **and** I go to the movie theater a lot.

More advanced connecting words at **B2 level** include:

- *because*, *since*, *as a result*, *due to* (these express cause and effect)
- *although*, *however*, *on the other hand* (these express contrast)

Examples:

- I'm running late **because** I missed my train.
- I'm going to the park, **and** I'm going to bring a picnic.
- **Since** I don't have any plans today, I can help you with your project.
- **As a result of** the heavy rain, the roads were flooded.
- **Due to** the power outage, the bank was closed all day.
- **Although** I like ice cream, I try not to eat too much of it.
- **However**, I think we should still give it a try.
- I'm not feeling well, **so** I won't be able to come to the party tonight.

B1: Future continuous

The future continuous is a verb tense used to describe an action that will be in progress at a specific time in the future. It is formed by combining the auxiliary verb *will* with the present participle *-ing*.

Examples:

- Tomorrow at 9 PM, I **will be studying** for my exam.
- Next year, they **will be traveling** the world.

The future continuous is used to talk about future actions that will be in progress, actions that will be happening when another action takes place, or actions that will last for a certain time in the future. It can also be used to express polite requests or to ask about future plans.

Examples:

- The party will be starting at 7 PM, so I**'ll be getting ready** soon.
- I**'ll be working** for the next hour, but I'll be free after that.
- **Will** you **be attending** the meeting tomorrow morning?

The future continuous is used only to talk about future actions, not present or past actions.

The question form: What **will** you **be doing** in five years' time?

The negative form: I **won't be going** to the shop.

EXERCISE

What will/won't you be doing in the future?

B1: Modals: *must, can't* (deduction)

Must and *can't* are modal verbs that are used to express deduction, or making a conclusion based on evidence or information.

Must is used to express a strong conclusion, meaning that something is probably true.

Example:

- She **must** be tired; she's been working all day.

Can't is used to express a negative conclusion, meaning that something is probably not true.

Example:

- He **can't** be home yet; his car is still not in the driveway.

Both *must* and *can't* are used to make conclusions about the present or future, but not the past. To make conclusions about the past, you would use the past tense form of the modal verb, such as *must have* or *couldn't have*[6].

Must and *can't* are not used for making deductions about the past unless you have evidence to support your conclusion. The use of these modal verbs should be used with caution, as they express a high degree of certainty, which may not always be accurate.

EXERCISE

Write five sentences using *must* and *can't*.

---

[6] See also the B1 entry for Modals: Should have, might have (past)

B1: Modals: *might, may, will* (and *probably*)

(See also the B1 entry for Will and going to – prediction*)*

The modal verbs *might, may, will,* and *probably* are auxiliary verbs used to express possibility, likelihood, or future actions.

Might and *may* are used to express possibility or uncertainty. **Might** is used to express a slightly lower level of possibility, whereas **may** expresses a higher level of possibility.

Examples:

- It **might** rain tomorrow.
- She **may** come to the party.

Will is used to express future actions or events that are certain to occur. *Will* is also used to express a strong intention or promise.

Examples:

- I **will** go to the store tomorrow.
- He **will** finish the work by the end of the week.

Probably is used to express an educated guess or a higher level of certainty.

Examples:

- She **is probably** at home.
- It **will probably** rain tomorrow.

EXERCISE

Write five sentences using *might, may, will,* and *probably*.

B1: Modals: *should have, might have,* etc. (past)

Should have, *might have*, and similar modal verbs are used to talk about past actions that could or should have happened, but didn't. These verbs are called "modal perfect" verbs because they combine the modal verb with *have* + past participle form of the main verb to talk about hypothetical past actions or events.

Examples:

- I **should have** studied harder for the exam, but I procrastinated. (regret about not taking action)
- She **might have** missed her flight if she didn't leave the house on time. (possibility or uncertainty about what happened in the past)
- They **will have** finished the project by the end of the week. (future in the past, meaning that by a certain point in the past, the action was completed)
- I **might have** gone to the party, but I was feeling tired. (uncertainty about what could have happened in the past)

EXERCISE

Write five sentences using *should have*, *will have*, and *might have*.

B1: Modals: *must, have to* (obligation)

Must and *have to* are modal verbs used to express obligation or necessity in English.

Must is used to express a strong obligation, often imposed by the speaker.

Example:

- "You **must** stop smoking."

Have to is used to express a milder obligation, often imposed by external circumstances.

Example:

- "You **have to** pay the bills."

Both *must* and *have to* can be used in the present and the past tense to indicate an obligation that existed at a particular time. In the negative form, *must not* (or *can't*) is used to indicate that something is forbidden, for example: "You must not park here." The negative form of *have to* is *don't have to*, which indicates that something is not necessary, for example: "You don't have to wear a suit."

Must is a modal verb that does not have a past participle form and thus cannot be used in the present perfect tense, whereas *have to* is a semi-modal verb that has a past participle form and can be used in the present perfect tense.

EXERCISE

Write five sentences using *must* and *have to*.

B1: Past perfect

The past perfect is a verb tense used to talk about actions or events completed before a certain point in the past. It is formed by combining the auxiliary verb *had* with the past participle of the main verb. For example, "I had eaten breakfast before I went to work."

The structure of the past perfect is: Subject + *had* + past participle of main verb.

The past perfect is often used in combination with the simple past to talk about sequences of events in the past, for example: "I had finished my work before I went to bed." It can also be used to show that an action was completed before a specific time in the past, for example: "By the time I arrived, the party had already started."

The past perfect is not used to describe the duration of an action in the past, but rather to talk about the completion of an action before another event or time in the past.

Other examples:

- I **had** already **eaten** breakfast when you called.
- They **had finished** the project before the deadline.
- She **had been** to Berlin twice before her trip last summer.
- The sun **had set** and it was dark outside.
- He **had learned** to play the guitar for a year before he started performing in public.
- We **had completed** the survey by the time the meeting started.
- The team **had won** three games in a row before losing their fourth match.
- I **had met** her once before our second meeting.
- The store **had closed** by the time we got there.

B1: Phrasal verbs (advanced)

(See also the A2 entry for Phrasal verbs; the teaching of phrasal verbs is recommended through to C2 level)

Phrasal verbs can be followed by more than one particle.

Examples:

- I'm trying to **cut down on** sugar and caffeine to improve my health.
- She **put up with** his behavior for years before finally leaving him.

Phrasal verbs can also be figurative (an abstract concept) or literal (a physical movement).

Examples:

- Phrasal verb: **Take off**

Figurative use: She's really **taken off** in her career, becoming one of the top executives in the company.

Literal use: I'm just going to **take off** my jacket.

- Phrasal verb: **Hold on**

Figurative use: We need to **hold on** to our values and principles, even in difficult times.

Literal use: Can you **hold on** to this package for me while I get my keys?

- Phrasal verb: **Set up**

Figurative use: The company is planning to **set up** a new division in Asia to expand their business.

Literal use: Can you help me **set up** the tent before it gets dark?

B1: Present perfect

The present perfect is used to talk about a past event that has some connection to the present. It is formed with *have/has* + past participle.

When past time is mentioned, the time is <u>not specific</u>.

Example:

- I **have visited** Athens three times (<u>in the past</u>).

We know this event happened in the past, but we don't know when exactly. The speaker's choice of present perfect here suggests that a) the speaker might visit Athens again in the future—that is, the action is finished forever; and b) the speaker is about to give more information about their experience of Athens.

The past simple, on the other hand, is used to talk about a completely finished event in the past. The time frame is a <u>finished</u> (period of) time. It is formed with the past tense of the verb.

Example:

- I **visited** Athens (<u>last year</u>). (*last year* is a completely finished time in the past)

The present perfect can also be used to talk about past experience across someone's lifetime.

Example:

- I have never been to New Zealand. (in my whole life)
- I've not been to New Zealand. (this is the same as the above sentence)
- He has flown in a helicopter. He flew in one last year.
- Have you ever met anyone famous?

---

1. Read the passage and underline the present perfect and the past simple tenses. Then say why each of those tenses were used.

Krista has always loved living in the city. She hasn't ever lived in the countryside. She walks to work every day, and she knows all of her neighbors. She often stops at the coffee shop on the corner for a latte on her way to the office. In fact, last week, she even went to the coffee shop on Saturday and Sunday. She has been working at the same job for five years now, and she enjoys it very much. She didn't enjoy it at first, but after her first year there, she started to enjoy it. Her boss is happy with her work, and she has made a lot of friends at the office. However, she has been thinking about making a change in her life. She has always wanted to travel, but she hasn't had the opportunity yet. She planned to take some time off work to explore the world. But that was in 2019, and then of course the pandemic happened. She has been researching different destinations and making plans for her trip. She hopes that she will be able to visit all of the places that she has always dreamed of seeing.

Answers: has ... loved, hasn't ... lived, went, didn't enjoy, started, has made, has ... wanted, hasn't had, planned, was, happened, has dreamed

2. Make some sentences about some of your past experiences.

B1: Present perfect continuous

The present perfect continuous (also known as the present perfect progressive) is a verb tense used to describe an action that started in the past and continues up to the present moment. It is formed using the auxiliary verb *has/have* + the present participle verb form *-ing*.

The present perfect continuous can help emphasize the duration of the action, especially if spoken with extra stress on the time phrase in the sentence. You will often see the time expressions *for* and *since* used with this tense.

Examples:

- I **have been studying** English for three years.
- They **have been playing** basketball for an hour.
- She **has been working** on this project for six months.
- They **haven't been going** out much since they retired.
- **Have** you **been eating** that cake?!

EXERCISE

Write five sentences that use the present perfect continuous.

1.

2.

3.

4.

5.

B1: Reported speech (indirect speech, range of tenses)

Reported speech (also known as indirect speech) refers to the reporting of what someone has said without using the exact words of the speaker. It's used to tell someone what someone else has said. In reported speech, the words of the speaker are usually changed to match the tense of the reporting verb.

Example:

"I **love** ice cream," said John. (direct speech) → John said that he **loves** ice cream. (indirect speech)

In the reported speech, the verb tense is changed to match the tense of the reporting verb *said*, which is past tense.

When reporting speech, the tense of the original speech may also change, as well as the person and pronouns. Additionally, the location and time expressions in may also need to be changed to reflect the time and place of the reporting, not the original speech.

Direct speech: "I**'m going** to the park today," said John. → Reported speech: John said that he **was going** to the park that day.

Direct speech: "I**'ll be here** at 10 o'clock tomorrow," said Soo. → Reported speech: Soo said that she **would be there** at 10 o'clock the next day.

Direct speech: "I **live** in Accra," said Tom. → Reported speech: Tom said that he **lived** in Accra.

("today" becomes "that day"; "tomorrow" becomes "the next day")

B1: Simple passive

(See also the B2 entry for Passive tenses*)*

The passive is a grammatical construction used to describe a situation or action where the focus is on the recipient of the action rather than the performer of the action. It is formed by using the auxiliary verb *be* + the past participle of the main verb.

Examples:

- The book **was written** by Jane Austen.

(The focus is on the book, which was written by Jane Austen.)

- The cake **is being baked** by my mother.

(The focus is on the cake, which is being baked by my mother now.)

- The museum **was visited** by thousands of tourists last year.

(The focus is on the museum, which was visited by thousands of tourists last year.)

Passive sentences often include **by** to indicate the agent (the performer of the action) of the sentence.

EXERCISE

Think of five pieces of artwork, books, or inventions. Say who was responsible for creating/writing/inventing them. Use the passive.

B1: *Used to*

Used to is used to talk about past habits, routines, and states that are no longer true in the present. *Used to* is followed by the base form of the verb (the infinitive without *to*).

Examples:

- I **used to** live in La Paz, but now I live in Mexico City.
- I **used to** play badminton a lot, but I don't anymore.

In the negative form, *used to* is accompanied by the verb *do*.

Note that in both the negative form and the question form, *used to* becomes *use to*.

Examples:

- I **didn't use to** like coffee, but now I love it.
- He **didn't use to** go there, but he now goes there a lot.
- **Did** you **use to** play the guitar?
- **Didn't** they **use to** go to this school?

Used to is often used with these past time expressions: *when I was younger*, *in the past*, or *back then*.

EXERCISE

Complete the sentences with *used to* and a suitable main verb.

1. When I was a child, I _____ cartoons every day.

2. My father _____ a pipe, but he quit when he was 50.

3. We _____ a cat, but now we have a dog.

4. Did she _____ the piano when she was younger?

5. They _____ in Bangkok, but now they do.

Answers: 1. used to watch; 2. used to smoke; 3. used to have; 4. use to play; 5. didn't use to

B1: *Wh-* questions in the past – reported speech

Wh- questions in the past are questions that start with words such as *who, what, where, when, why,* and *how,* and ask about past events or situations. In the past tense, these questions are formed using the appropriate auxiliary verb, such as *did,* in the simple past tense. In reported speech, the subject pronoun and verb also change to match the tense.

Examples:

- **Direct speech:** "What did you eat for breakfast?"
- **Reported speech:** She asked me what I had eaten for breakfast.
- **Direct speech:** "Where did you go on vacation?"
- **Reported speech:** He asked me where I had gone on vacation.

It's important to pay attention to the time expressions and make necessary changes to match the tense of the reporting verb.

EXERCISE

Ask the questions to someone and then report back what they said.

1. What did you do yesterday evening?

2. Where did you eat lunch?

3. Why did you want to study English?

4. Who did you see last weekend?

5. When was the last time you ate ice-cream?

6. Which popstar was your favorite when you were younger?

B1: *Will* and *going* to – prediction

(See also the A2 entry for Future time *[will* and *going to]*)

Apart from their use to express future plans, *will* and *going to* are also used to express future predictions.

Will is used to make a prediction based on less concrete evidence (i.e., the situation has a medium to high-medium chance of happening).

Examples of use for predictions:

- I think it'll rain later, so I'll take my umbrella. (Possible context: The speaker has seen a forecast for rain for that morning, so is guessing that rain will follow in the afternoon as well. It is a stronger guess than with using *might*.)
- It looks like there'll be trouble. (Possible context: The speaker can see two people having a serious disagreement at work, so predicts a future problem. It is a stronger guess than with using *might*.)

Going to is used to make a prediction based on present evidence (i.e., the situation has a high chance of happening).

Examples of use for prediction:

- She's **going to** fall. (Possible context: The speaker can see an old lady who is looking unsteady as she carries a heavy bag down some steps.)
- It's **going to** be a disaster. (Possible context: The speaker predicts that an event will have a bad outcome because lots of things are going wrong in the run up to the event.)

B2: Future perfect

The future perfect tense is used to talk about a completed action in the future. It's formed by combining the auxiliary verb *will* + the past participle of the main verb.

Example:

- I **will have eaten** breakfast by 8 AM.

In this example, the future perfect tense is used to describe an action that will have been completed by a specific time in the future. The future perfect tense is often used to express a sense of certainty about an event that will happen in the future.

Examples:

- By next year, I **will have lived** in this city for 10 years.
- She **will have finished** her degree when she turns 25.
- The train **will have arrived** before we get to the station.

The future perfect tense is not used to talk about ongoing or continuous actions. Instead, it's used to describe a completed action at a specific point in the future.

Complete the sentences using the future perfect tense.

1. By this time next year, I _____ (finish) my degree.

2. She _____ (read) that book by the end of the week.

3. They _____ (travel) to six different countries by the time they return home.

4. He _____ (complete) the project before the deadline.

5. I _____ (exercise) for an hour by the time you arrive.

6. The movie _____ (start) by the time we get there.

7. By the end of this month, we _____ (save) enough money for our trip.

8. They _____ (prepare) dinner by the time we get home.

9. She _____ (paint) her room before she moves in.

10. By the time I turn 30, I _____ (visit) every continent.

Answers: 1. will have finished; 2. will have read; 3. will have traveled/travelled; 4. will have completed; 5. will have exercised; 6. will have started; 7. will have saved; 8. will have prepared; 9. will have painted; 10. will have visited

B2: Future perfect continuous

The future perfect continuous tense is used to describe an action that will have been happening continuously up until a specific time in the future. It is formed by using the auxiliary verb *will* + *have* + *been* + present participle (*-ing*).

Examples:

- By next year, I **will have been studying** English for 10 years.
- By the end of the week, she **will have been working** in that department for one year.
- They **will have been living** in that house for 25 years by the time they retire.

Question and negative forms do exist with this tense, but they are not commonly used, because the purpose of this tense tends to be to emphasize how long someone has been doing something— often a long time.

EXERCISES

1. Write five sentences about you that use the future perfect continuous tense.

1.

2.

3.

4.

5.

2. Complete the sentences using the future perfect continuous tense.

1. By 6 PM tonight, I _____ (study) for 3 hours.

2. By next month, she _____ (work) on this project for six months.

3. By the time we arrive, they _____ (wait) for us for two hours.

4. By the end of this week, he _____ (practice) his guitar for 10 hours.

5. By the time I reach home, she _____ (cook) dinner for four hours.

6. By the time we leave, the band _____ (perform) for three hours.

7. By the end of the year, we _____ (live) in this city for 5 years.

8. By the time we finish the game, they _____ (play) for two hours.

9. By next month, he _____ (learn) French for six months.

10. By the time the concert ends, they _____ (sing) for three hours.

Answers: 1. will have been studying; 2. will have been working; 3. will have been waiting; 4. will have been practicing; 5. will have been cooking; 6. will have been performing; 7. will have been living; 8. will have been playing; 9. will have been learning; 10. will have been singing

B2: Mixed conditionals

A mixed conditional sentence is a sentence that combines elements of two different types of conditional sentences to express an imaginary situation in the present or future, and its possible result.

Examples:

- **If I had studied** harder, I <u>would have passed</u> the exam. (a combination of a past hypothetical situation with a future result)
- **If** she **drinks** too much coffee, she <u>will be unable to sleep</u> tonight. (a combination of a present hypothetical situation with a future result)

The structure of a mixed conditional sentence typically follows this pattern: *If* + past perfect, *would/could/might* + present simple.

Note that the use of past perfect in the *if* clause reflects the hypothetical situation, while the modal verbs in the result clause express the likelihood of the outcome. The order of the clauses can be switched. A comma is needed when the *if* clause comes first.

Example:

- **If I had studied** harder, I <u>would have passed</u> the exam.
- I <u>would have passed</u> the exam **if I had studied** harder.

Complete the conditional sentences.

1. If I _____ (study) more, I _____ in a better position now.

2. If you _____ (move) quickly, you _____ there sooner.

3. If it _____ (not rain), we _____ for a walk.

4. If you _____ (tell) me earlier, I _____ you.

5. If we _____ (leave) sooner, we _____ in traffic now.

Answers: 1. If I had studied more, I would be in a better position now.; 2. If you move quickly, you will get there sooner.; 3. If it wasn't raining, we would go for a walk.; 4. If you had told me earlier, I would have helped you.; 5. If we had left sooner, we wouldn't be stuck in traffic now.

B2: Modals: *needn't have*

Needn't have is a modal verb that is used to talk about actions that were not necessary in the past, but were thought to be necessary. This modal verb is used to show that the speaker realizes, after the fact, that an action was not necessary. It is often used in negative sentences to express regret or disappointment about something that has already happened. For example:

- I **needn't have** worried about the test. I passed easily.
- I **needn't have** brought an umbrella. It didn't rain after all.

In these examples, the speaker is expressing regret about actions that were not necessary. The first sentence expresses regret about worrying about the test, and the second sentence expresses regret about bringing an umbrella.

EXERCISE

Write five sentences that use *needn't have*.

B2: Modals of deduction and speculation

Modal verbs of deduction and speculation (i.e., guessing what you think has happened / will happen) are used to express the speaker's degree of certainty or uncertainty about a situation or event. These modal verbs include *must*, *may*, *might*, *could*, and *can't*.

Examples:

- She **must** be late, her train was delayed. (deduction)
- He **may** be sick, he hasn't answered any of my calls. (speculation)
- It **might** rain later, the sky is getting cloudy. (speculation)
- She **could** be lost, she hasn't arrived yet. (speculation)
- They **can't** be on vacation, they said they would be back today. (deduction)

EXERCISE

Write three sentences of deduction, and three sentences of speculation.

B2: Narrative tenses

Narrative tenses are the set of verb tenses used to tell a story or describe events that happen in a sequence over time. The three most common narrative tenses in English are:

Past simple: Used to describe completed actions in the past. There can be added detail about the surrounding context at the time of the completed action.

Examples:

- He **walked** to the store.
- He **walked** to the store in the rain.

Past continuous: Used to describe an ongoing action that was in progress in the past. Another action could start during the first action.

Examples:

- He **was walking** to the store.
- He **was walking** to the store, <u>when</u> it **started** to rain. (the action of walking started before the rain started)

Past perfect: Used to describe actions that were completed before another action in the past.

Example:

- He **had walked** to the store <u>before</u> it **started** to rain. (the person was at the store when the rain started)

EXERCISE

Narrate events about something that happened to you.

B2: Passive tenses

(See also the B1 entry for Simple passive*)*

The passive is made of the verb *to be* + past participle. There are different passive tenses.

Simple passive: The window **was broken** by the wind.

Past continuous passive: The letter **was being written** by him at that time.

Past perfect passive: The cake **had been baked** by the time we arrived.

Present perfect passive: The project **has been completed** by the team.

Present continuous passive: The house **is being painted** by the workers.

Future simple passive: The report **will be submitted** by the end of the week.

Future continuous passive: The roads **will be being repaired** by this time next week.

Future perfect passive: The book **will have been read** by the time you come back.

Future perfect continuous passive: The garden **will have been being tended** to for a year by next summer.

B2: Past perfect continuous

The past perfect continuous is a tense used to describe an action that was in progress and ongoing up until a certain point in the past. It is formed using the auxiliary verb *had* + *been* + present participle (*-ing*). The past participle is used to describe the state or activity of the subject, which is in progress and goes on for an extended period of time in the past.

Examples:

- I **had been working** on the project for hours when my computer crashed.
- They **had been studying** for their exams for weeks and were exhausted by the time they finally took them.
- She **had been dating** Jin for a month when they broke up.

EXERCISE

Complete the sentences using the past perfect continuous tense.

1. He _____ (study) for three hours when his friends arrived.

2. They _____ (wait) for two hours before the train finally arrived.

3. By the time we got to the restaurant, the chef _____ (cook) for six hours.

4. She _____ (walk) for two hours when she realized she was lost.

5. By the time they got home, the kids _____ (play) outside for three hours.

Answers: 1. had been studying; 2. had been waiting; 3. had been cooking; 4. had been walking; 5. had been playing

B2: Relative clauses

Relative clauses are clauses that add additional information to a sentence. They are often introduced by relative pronouns such as *who, whom, whose, that,* and *which.*

Examples:

- The man **who is speaking to the group** is my boss.
- The book, **which I read last night**, was very interesting.
- The woman **whose car broke down** needs a ride.
- The company **that I work for** is based in Bangalore.

Defining (= restrictive) relative clauses are usually essential for the understanding of the sentence and cannot be removed. In the following sentence, the speaker wants to include essential information for the listener about a specific mistake:

- The mistake **that caused the accident** involved using the wrong glue at the point of manufacture.

Relative clauses can also be **non-defining (= non-restrictive)**, providing additional but non-essential information about the noun. Non-defining relative clauses are often set off by commas.

Examples:

- Mustafa, **who is a doctor**, is my neighbor. (it's not essential for the listener to know that Mustafa is a doctor)
- The city, **which is famous for its architecture**, is Paris. (it's not essential for the listener to hear that Paris is famous for its architecture—maybe they know that fact already)

At C1 level, you will find *which* paired with prepositions. For example: *in which, of which, below which, near which, upon which,* etc.

Complete the sentences with an appropriate relative pronoun.

1. The movie _____ we saw last night was really scary.

2. The girl _____ mother is a doctor is in my class.

3. The book _____ I'm reading is about the history of the internet.

4. The car _____ we rented for our vacation was very comfortable.

5. The teacher _____ taught me English was very patient.

6. The restaurant _____ we went to last night had amazing food.

7. The woman _____ house we visited is a famous actress.

8. The dog _____ barked at me was very friendly.

9. The man _____ we met at the party is a famous author.

10. The city _____ we visited last summer was very beautiful.

Answers: 1. that; 2. whose; 3. that/which; 4. that/which; 5. who/that; 6. that/which; 7. whose; 8. that/which; 9. whom/who/that; 10. that/which

B2: Reported speech (indirect speech, questions)

Reported speech questions in English are used when we want to report what someone has asked us. In reported speech, we change the tense, pronouns, and sometimes other words used in the original question to reflect the speaker's perspective.

When reporting a question, we usually use the verb *ask* or *wonder* followed by an object pronoun (me, him, her, us, them) or the noun that the person asked the question to.

Examples:

Direct speech: "Where are you going?"

Reported speech: She asked me where I was going.

Direct speech: "What time is it?"

Reported speech: He wondered what time it was.

Direct speech: "Did you finish your homework?"

Reported speech: They asked if I had finished my homework.

Direct speech: "How long have you been studying?"

Reported speech: She asked me how long I had been studying.

In reported speech, we use the appropriate tense of the verb *to be* and often use *if* or *whether* to introduce the question.

Direct speech: "Where is your sister?"

Reported speech: He asked me where his sister was.

Direct speech: "Have you seen my phone?"

Reported speech: She asked if I had seen her phone.

Direct speech: "Can I help you?"

Reported speech: The receptionist asked if she could help me.

B2: *Wish*

Wish is a modal verb used to express a desire or a hope for something to happen or be different. It can also be used to express regret or to talk about an imaginary situation. The structure of the verb *wish* varies with the tense used, as well as the subject of the sentence.

The basic structure of the verb *wish* is: Subject + *wish* + (that) + past tense verb

Examples:

- I **wish I had** a bigger house. (expressing regret)
- I **wish it would** stop raining. (expressing a desire)
- She **wishes she could** speak French fluently. (talking about an imaginary situation)

The word *that* can be omitted in the sentence. The past tense verb following the word *wish* should be in the simple past, past continuous, past perfect or past perfect continuous, depending on the meaning you want to express.

EXERCISE

Write three sentences using *wish*.

1.

2.

3.

B2: *Would* – habits in the past

(See also the B1 entry for Used to*)*

The modal verb *would* can be used to express habits or repeated actions in the past. When used in this way, it has a similar meaning to *used to*, but *would* is more formal. The verb that follows *would* is in the infinitive form (without *to*).

Examples:

- When I was a child, I **would** always <u>play</u> outside with my friends after school.
- Every summer, my family **would** <u>go</u> to the beach for a week.
- I **would** <u>read</u> a book before going to bed every night.
- **Would** you <u>fall asleep</u> easily when you were a teenager?
- They **wouldn't** <u>go</u> there alone when they were little children, **would** they?

EXERCISE

Write three sentences using *would*.

1.

2.

3.

C1: Inversion with negative adverbials

Inversion is a grammatical structure in which the subject and auxiliary verb of a clause are switched in order to place emphasis on the auxiliary verb or to create a more formal or stylistically marked tone. Negative adverbials are adverbs or adverbial phrases that express negation, such as *never, not, nothing, no one*.

When a negative adverbial is present, inversion can occur by placing the auxiliary verb before the subject.

Examples:

- **Never** <u>have I seen</u> such a beautiful sunset.
- **Not until** the next morning <u>did they realize</u> their mistake.

This type of inversion is known as negative inversion, and it is often used in formal writing, literary language, and in certain idiomatic expressions.

Other examples:

- Never before had she felt so nervous.
- Rarely does she attend concerts.
- Seldom had she seen such beauty.
- Hardly had he finished the project when he realized he made a mistake.
- Only after the storm had passed did they venture outside.
- Under no circumstances would he compromise his beliefs.
- At no time did they consider giving up.
- In no way was he prepared for the outcome.
- Nowhere had they seen such a magnificent sunset.
- Not until the sun had set did they realize how late it was getting.

C1: Mixed conditionals in past, present, future

Mixed conditionals combine *two different* conditional structures to express a hypothetical situation and its outcome.

Examples:

- **If** she **had studied** harder, she would have passed the exam. (past hypothetical outcome based on **past** hypothetical condition)
- **If** he **keeps** eating junk food, he will get sick. (future hypothetical outcome based on **present** hypothetical condition)
- **If** it **rains** tomorrow, I would stay home. (future hypothetical outcome based on **future** hypothetical condition)
- **If** they **had invested** in the stock market back then, they would be rich now. (present hypothetical outcome based on **past** hypothetical condition)
- **If** he **studies** more, he could pass the exam. (future hypothetical outcome based on **present** hypothetical condition)

The different tenses used in mixed conditionals can change the meaning of the sentences and express different degrees of uncertainty.

Complete the sentences using mixed conditional sentences in the past, present, or future.

1. If I _____ (win) the lottery last year, I _____ (have) bought a new car.

2. If you _____ (study) harder in high school, you _____ (get) into a better university.

3. If he _____ (not leave) the house without his keys, he _____ (not get) locked out.

4. If we _____ (go) to bed earlier, we _____ (feel) more rested in the morning.

5. If they _____ (not invest) in stocks, they _____ (not make) a profit.

6. If she _____ (get) the job, she _____ (move) to a new city.

7. If you _____ (not take) care of your health, you _____ (have) health problems in the future.

8. If the weather _____ (be) nice tomorrow, we _____ (go) to the beach.

9. If they _____ (have) more time, they _____ (travel) the world.

10. If he _____ (be) more careful, he _____ (not break) his leg.

Answers: 1. If I had won the lottery last year, I would have bought a new car.; 2. If you had studied harder in high school, you would have gotten into a better university.; 3. If he had not left the house without his keys, he would not have gotten locked out.; 4. If we go to bed earlier, we will feel more rested in the morning.; 5. If they had not invested in stocks, they would not have made a profit.; 6. If she gets the job, she will move to a new city.; 7. If you do not take care of your health, you will have health problems in the future.; 8. If the weather is nice tomorrow, we will go to the beach.; 9. If they had more time, they would travel the world.; 10. If he had been more careful, he would not have broken his leg.

C1: Modals in the past

Modal verbs are auxiliary verbs that are used to express modality, which is the speaker's attitude or opinion about the likelihood, ability, permission, or obligation related to the action of the main verb. When used in the past, modal verbs indicate past possibility, past ability, past permission, past obligation, past prediction, past deduction, or past speculation.

The past forms of the modal verbs are:

- could (have)
- might have
- must have
- had to
- ought to have
- should have
- would (have)[7]

Examples:

- **Past possibility:** She **could have** gone to her uncle's house—she said she might visit him.
- **Past ability:** He **could** speak six languages fluently.
- **Past permission:** They **could** stay up late on weekends.
- **Past obligation:** She **had to** finish her homework before she watched TV.
- **Past prediction:** I thought it **would** rain, so I brought an umbrella.
- **Past deduction (strong possibility):** She **must have** gone to bed early, because she wasn't at the party.
- **Past speculation (high uncertainty):** They **may have** missed the train, or the train **might have** had some technical problems, because they didn't show up.

---

[7] See also the B2 entry for Would – habits in the past

Complete the sentences using an appropriate past modal verb with a main verb.

1. I was sick last week, so I _____ to work.

2. My car broke down, so I _____ to the meeting on time.

3. The movie was really boring, so we _____ it.

4. I wasn't sure what the answer to the question was, so I _____ it correctly.

5. She didn't have enough money, so she _____ the concert ticket.

6. He is wearing a medal, so he _____ the race.

7. We had a map, so we _____ to find our way back to the hotel.

8. They only had bread, so they _____ that.

9. She had a headache, so she _____ all day for her exam.

10. The weather was terrible, so we _____ to the beach.

Possible answers: 1. I was sick last week, so I couldn't go to work.; 2. My car broke down, so I couldn't get to the meeting on time.; 3. The movie was really boring, so we couldn't enjoy it.; 4. I wasn't sure what the answer to the question was, so I might not have answered it correctly.; 5. She didn't have enough money, so she couldn't buy the concert ticket. 6. He is wearing a medal, so he must have finished the race.; 7. We had a map, so we ought to have been able to find our way back to the hotel.; 8. They only had bread, so they had to eat that. 9. She had a headache, so she might not have studied for her exam.; 10. The weather was terrible, so we couldn't go to the beach.

C1: Phrasal verbs, especially splitting

Phrasal verbs (also called multi-word verbs) consist of a main verb and one or two particles. The particles are usually adverbials or prepositions. In English, some phrasal verbs can be split, meaning that the verb and particle(s) can be separated by other words.

Examples:

- I **turned off** the lights. (note: *turn off* is an intransitive verb, meaning it must take an object [the lights])
- I **turned** the lights **off**.
- I **turned** them **off**.

EXERCISE

Underline the phrasal verbs, and identify:

a) What do the verbs in the sentence mean?

b) Can they be split or not?

1. She looked up the information for me.

2. I will put back the book on the shelf later.

3. He ran into his old friend at the store.

4. Can you turn off the music?

5. She took off her coat and hung it up.

Answers: 1. a) looked up = researched, b) yes; 2. a) put back = return, b) yes; 3. a) ran into = met by chance, b) no; 4. a) turn off = switch off, b) yes; 5. a) took off = remove, hung (it) up = put on a hook, b) no

C1: *Wish/If only* – regrets

The verbs *wish* and *if only* are used to express regrets about the past or present.

Examples:

- <u>I wish</u> I **hadn't forgotten** my keys. (regret about the past)
- <u>If only</u> I **had listened** to her advice. (regret about the past)
- <u>I wish</u> I **wasn't** so busy today. (regret about the present)
- <u>If only</u> I **could** take the day off. (regret about the present)

These expressions are usually used to express a desire for things to be different, or a regret about a decision that has been made. These expressions don't change the situation they are describing, they are simply a way of expressing disappointment or frustration.

EXERCISE

Change the sentences to use *wish* or *not only*.

1. I regret not traveling more when I was younger.

2. I regret not learning another language.

3. I regret not saving money when I had the chance.

4. I regret not taking better care of my health.

5. I not only regret quitting my job, but I also regret not having a plan B.

Answers: 1. I wish I had traveled more when I was younger.; 2. If only I had learned another language.; 3. I wish I had saved money when I had the chance.; 4. If only I had taken better care of my health.; 5. Not only do I regret quitting my job, but I also regret not having a plan B.

List of English verb tenses

Here is a list of all the tenses in English grammar, categorized by their aspect* (simple, continuous, perfect, perfect continuous).

Simple aspect:

- Present simple - I eat breakfast every day.
- Past simple - I watched a movie last night.
- Future simple - I will visit my parents next week.

Continuous aspect:

- Present continuous - I am watching TV right now.
- Past continuous - I was playing football when it started raining.
- Future continuous - I will be studying for my exam at this time tomorrow.

Perfect aspect:

- Present perfect - I have visited Paris twice.
- Past perfect - I had finished my work before he arrived.
- Future perfect - I will have graduated by next year.

Perfect continuous (progressive) aspect:

- Present perfect continuous - I have been studying for three hours.
- Past perfect continuous - I had been waiting for two hours before he came.
- Future perfect continuous - I will have been working here for 10 years by the end of next month.

* "Aspect" is not the same as "tense." *Aspect* refers to how an action or event is viewed in terms of its completion (perfect), duration, repetition, or ongoing (continuous/progressive) nature. *Tense*, on the other hand, is about the time of the action or event (past, present, or future).

List of English verbs: past simple, past participle

These common English verbs are listed here in the order of their infinitive form (dictionary form), past simple form, and their past participle (used in the present perfect tense).

- be (infinitive) - was/were (past simple) – been (past participle)
- have - had - had
- do - did - done
- say - said - said
- get - got - gotten/got
- make - made - made
- go - went - gone
- know - knew - known
- take - took - taken
- see - saw - seen
- come - came - come
- think - thought - thought
- look - looked - looked
- want - wanted - wanted
- give - gave - given
- use - used - used
- find - found - found
- tell - told - told
- work - worked - worked
- call - called – called

List of English pronouns

Personal pronouns				
Subject pronouns	Object pronouns	Possessive adjectives	Possessive pronouns	Reflexive pronouns
I	me	my	mine	myself
you	you	your	yours	yourself
he	him	his	his	himself
she	her	her	hers	herself
it	it	its	its	itself
we	us	our	ours	ourselves
you	you	your	yours	yourselves
they	them	their	theirs	themselves

Demonstrative pronouns: this, that, these, those

Interrogative pronouns: who, whom, whose, what, which

Relative pronouns: who, whom, whose, whoever, whomever, which, that

Indefinite pronouns: anyone, anything, someone, something, everyone, everything, nobody, no one, nothing, both, few, many, several, others, several, all, any, none, some[8]

Reciprocal pronouns: each other, one another

---

[8] Some words, such as *some* and *any*, can function as either indefinite pronouns or as determiners, depending on the context in which they are used.

American English grammar vs other varieties

There are a few differences between American English grammar and the grammar of other English-speaking countries. These differences are going to be more important for a user who needs to use English in a professional context, but learners will not be tested whether they know them in standard English exams. The differences include:

Verb agreement: In American English, collective nouns are usually treated as singular, whereas in British English, they can be treated as singular or plural depending on the context or the speaker's personal choice.

- The team is playing well. (American)
- The team is/are playing well. (British)

Prepositions: In some cases, British English uses different prepositions than American English.

- I'm walking in the street. (American)
- I'm walking on the street. (British)

Tense usage: British English sometimes uses the present perfect tense where American English would use the past simple tense.

- I just had breakfast. (American)
- I've just had breakfast. (British)

Irregular verbs: Some verbs have different past tense or spelling forms in American and British English.

- I dove into the pool. (American)
- I dived into the pool. (British)
- I learned to play the guitar. (American)
- I learnt to play the guitar. (British)

Teaching activities to help learners practice the past tenses

Timeline activity: Draw a timeline on the board or a sheet of paper, and label it with the present, past, and future. Ask learners to come up with sentences using different past tense and to place them on the timeline in the correct order.

Storytelling: Have learners work in pairs or small groups to create a story using different past tenses. Each group can then share their story with the class, and the class can recount parts of the story and discuss which past tenses were used and why.

Error correction: Give learners a text or paragraph that contains errors in past tenses and have them work in pairs to identify and correct the errors. This can help learners develop their self-editing skills.

Video activity: Show a video or a movie clip and ask learners to write a summary using either the past simple or present perfect tense.

Board game: Create a board game with different squares that require the use of different past tense sentences. Learners can work in pairs or groups to play the game and use the tenses.

Project: Learners can work independently or in groups to create a presentation or a short video that explains an English past tense.

Further reading and tips about learning grammar

At the time of writing, there were some 80,000+ search results for "grammar books" on Amazon. Clearly, the choice is overwhelming. In my view, you need to choose a book that's right for your learning style.

If you are looking for the most established and extensive grammar reference books, I recommend these:

- *English Grammar in Use* [various levels] – by R. Murphy (Cambridge University Press)
- *Grammar for English Language Teachers* – by M. Parrott (Cambridge University Press)
- *Practical English Grammar* – by M. Swan (Oxford University Press)

There are also lots of free grammar resources available online. Some of the well-known ones with a large amount of content include the websites of the British Council (https://learnenglish.britishcouncil.org/grammar), the BBC's Learning English (https://www.bbc.co.uk/learningenglish/basic-grammar), and Education First (https://www.ef.co.uk/english-resources/english-grammar/). Elsewhere, many universities will have webpages on grammar usage.

There are also plenty of YouTube videos on English grammar.

Most importantly, I would suggest you don't fixate on learning/teaching the metalanguage around grammar. For example, outside of a grammar book, phrases such as "the preterite" and "present perfect continuous" will have limited use. And, why is the past "perfect"? Also, grammar "rules" taught in books often have many exceptions when language is used naturally. I recommend viewing grammar as "patterns" that you notice in (example) sentences.

From my observations of English learners over the years, the key to being successful in English is to have confidence and use English as much as possible. I know that some countries place a lot of value on prioritizing the teaching of grammar rules (this is perhaps a legacy of the fixation of mastering Latin grammatical structures by the elite in times gone by), but even if grammar rules are emphasized from the outset, it's really only those who actively use the language who go on to be good.

Printed in Great Britain
by Amazon

25597531R00069